A

Illust

Edited by Jill Holley

Acknowledgments:
Pam Roberts & Cyril Trenfield
(Ramblers' Association)

Central Library, Bristol
Dawn Hill
Frank Clarke
Kay Borman
Chris Cowley
John Davis
Monica Davis

© *Illustrations:* Lorraine Orriss, *Text:* Graham Hoyle 2000

Published by:
Graham Hoyle

Printed by:
Bookcraft Ltd, Midsomer Norton

All profits to the Samaritans

ISBN: 0–9537767–0–0

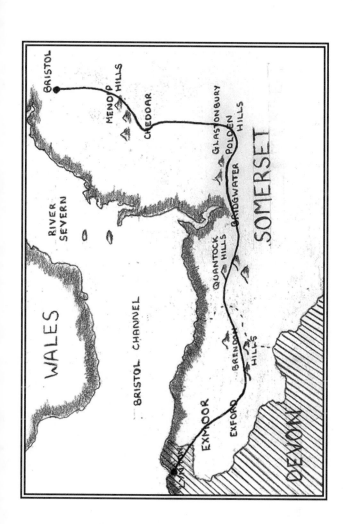

A WALK FROM BRISTOL

CLIFTON to LYNTON
(BRISTOL TO THE SEA)

A WALK ENCOMPASSING ONE HUNDRED AND THIRTY MILES
OF MAGNIFICENT ENGLISH COUNTRYSIDE - VALLEYS, HILLS,
LEVELS, MOORLANDS AND VILLAGES, CULMINATING IN THE
SPECTACULAR SCENERY OF THE COASTAL PATH

This is an ideal link path between the Cotswold Way and the North
Devon Coastal Path. The sixteen miles bridging the walks between
Bath and Bristol is on a well-established footpath, much of which
runs along the banks of the River Avon. This book covers in detail
the one hundred miles from Bristol to Lynton in Devon.

The last thirty miles of the journey, from Lynton to Croyde Bay,
provides an interesting addition, with a very good stretch of coastal
path nearly all of, which is the property of the National Trust, thus
avoiding the hazards of caravan parks, etc. Several books detailing
this area have already been written, so the description will only be
brief. The coastal path is extremely well waymarked and easy to
follow.

Should you be fortunate enough to have a couple of weeks to spare,
there will be ample time to cover the walk. If you only have one
week then it is best to set off on a Saturday from Bristol. The city is
easily accessible to outsiders, as it is served by good train and coach
transport.

Ideally, you should arrive in Bristol on a Friday evening, have an overnight stay in bed and breakfast or Youth Hostel accommodation, and arrive at Clifton Suspension Bridge early next morning to start the walk, aiming to complete it on the following Saturday afternoon. This should allow you plenty of time to travel by bus from Croyde Bay to Barnstaple, then by coach or train home.

Don't forget to check bus and train timetable details, as these do vary during the seasons. Also check that Youth Hostels are open on your chosen day.

Now for a little geographical detail about the areas surrounding the walk.

Ninety-three miles of the walk is in Somerset. The county resembles an elbow, fitting snugly around Bridgwater Bay in the Bristol Channel. It is cushioned by its neighbouring counties of Devon, Dorset, Wiltshire and Gloucestershire, only broken by Bristol, a city and county in its own right for over 600 years with a brief interruption of approximately twenty one years before the boundaries were reinstated.

The walk will take you through the L-shaped county with its great variety of scenery: from Bristol to Long Ashton, up and over the slopes of Dundry, at the top of which one can see as far as the Cotswold hills. Then across the Chew Valley with its peaceful lake and attractive villages, and on over the Mendip hills to Cheddar, famous for its cheese, the Gorge and the rare Cheddar Pink, which flowers on its crags around June.

From the Mendips, move on across the Somerset Levels to historic Glastonbury with its Abbey and Tor, on which is the tower of St Michael's Chapel. Next to the village of Street, with the Shoe Museum and then along the Polden Hills with views of the Somerset

Levels. You will pass through Bridgwater and on to the Quantock Hills with a spectacular ridge path, before dropping down into the villages around the Brendon Hills.

The next stage of the walk will take you across the Exmoor National Park, known for its wild ponies and one of the very few environments in England where the wild red deer may be found. After leaving Exford village, you will walk over the roof of Exmoor and down into the Doone Valley and Badgworthy Water, which feature in R. D. Blackmore's novel "Lorna Doone".

Moving further on along the East Lyn River you arrive at Watersmeet, where the Rivers Lyn and Hoaroak Water meet, then a steep climb takes you up into Myrtleberry Cleaves. As you progress through the Cleaves, glance to your right. You have arrived at the sea, and Lynton, a worthy ending to the one hundred-mile link path from Bristol.

At this point you may decide to end your journey. Should you decide to continue for the next thirty miles to Croyde Bay you will not be disappointed.

MAPS

In order to avoid infringement of Copyright Laws, which limit the use of maps less than 50 years old, the book utilises Ordnance Survey maps of approximately 1938 edition.

The map scale used is not completely consistent throughout the book, although the greater part of the route is depicted at approximately one and a half inches to the mile, with direction North always at the top of the page. Sections of the map have been produced on a larger scale giving a little more detail where difficulties may be found.

Youth Hostels (YH), and also various towns and villages on route where refreshment and rest may be taken, are marked with their mileage from Bristol. e.g. "Cheddar 20".

It is advisable when embarking on this walk to be equipped with a compass and relevant Ordnance Survey maps, as listed. By using the public rights of way the walker should be able to proceed unhindered (a few minor obstacles have been taken up with the Local Authorities and will in time be cleared).

A key to map reading has been purposely omitted, for the route map can easily be followed when used in conjunction with the written description of the journey.

No responsibility can be taken for any directional or descriptive error, but every endeavour has been made to avoid this.

RECOMMENDED ORDNANCE SURVEY MAPS

1 1/4 inches to the mile

1:50000 Landranger Series: SHEETS: 172, 182, 181, 180.

2 1/2 inches to the mile

1:25000 Explorer Series: Sheets : 154, 141, 140, 139 and

Outdoor Leisure Map No 9

or alternatively:

1:25000 Pathfinder series		
	1166	1236
	1182	1235
	1198	1215
	1218	1214
	1238	1213
	1237	

Conversion Chart

Miles	Kilometres	Miles	Kilometres
1	1.61	20	32.19
2	3.22	30	48.28
3	4.83	40	64.37
4	6.44	50	80.47
5	8.05	60	96.56
6	9.66	70	112.65
7	11.27	80	128.75
8	12.88	90	144.84
9	14.48	100	160.93
10	16.09		

DIVIDED SECTIONS

1). BRISTOL to CHEDDAR: 20 miles
   Chew Valley and Mendip Hills

2). CHEDDAR to BRIDGWATER: 29 miles
   Somerset Levels, Polden Hills and Villages

3). BRIDGWATER to LUXBOROUGH: 25 miles
   Quantock Hills and Brendon Villages

4). LUXBOROUGH to - LYNTON: 26 miles
   Exmoor, Doone Valley and Cleaves

5). LYNTON to CROYDE BAY: 30 miles
   Coastal Path with Ilfracombe and Combe Martin

All sections can be split to suit the walker's requirements.

BRISTOL to CHEDDAR - 20 MILES

Chew Valley and the Mendip Hills

Start the walk by crossing the Clifton Suspension Bridge, O/S 172, G.R.566732. Looking across to the left you will see Dundry Tower, which is the first major landmark, about four and a half miles away. Having crossed the Bridge, walk straight on up the road. Take care crossing the busy Portishead Road, and enter through the gatehouse into Ashton Court Estate.

N.B. The gates of the Estate open from 8.00 a.m. (when it becomes a public right of way) to dusk. If you wish to start earlier in the morning, you would need to skirt around the Ashton Court Estate by turning left after leaving the Suspension Bridge and into Burwalls Road, eventually finishing up at Long Ashton.

Having entered the Estate, continue along the drive. When you start to drop down, you will see the Domesday Oak on your left, supported by props. Further on, there is a Deer Park on the right. The drive then winds down left towards Ashton Court Mansion. Do not turn right at the end of the deer park, but continue to the next junction, bear right and leave the Estate by the gate on the South side. Taking great care, cross over the Clevedon road into Long Ashton and continue up the road until you reach the Angel Inn. After the Inn, turn left down Church Lane. With the Church on your left, go through the churchyard and pass through a gate into a field on the right. Keep close to the right hand boundary, cross over two stiles, continue over two more fields, going over two stiles, and then bear left to a small stream and over a footbridge. After the footbridge turn right, keeping close to the stream, then go over a stile and arrive in Yanley Lane. Turn left, go underneath the Long Ashton Bypass, and also the railway bridge, then continue along the lane until you reach a junction. Bear left at the junction, keeping to the main lane.

Keep straight on for about one mile until you reach the busy A38. Again take care, and cross straight over into Yanleigh Close, at the top of which there is a footpath. A few yards up here, go over a stile into a field. Keep straight ahead, and cross another stile. Still walking in the same direction, go through a gateway, up the field and on to a stile. Continue up towards some farm buildings. Pass through a gate and go down the farm track, turning right when you reach the road. Keep right at the next junction of lanes, and soon on the left you will see some bungalows. At the side of the second bungalow take a track on the left, then cross a stile into a field. Turn right, following the hedge on your right, and go over the next stile. Still follow the right hand boundary. Go over a stile in the corner. Continue on, then up some steps to meet the road. Turn left and proceed uphill.

On reaching the village of Dundry, turn right and go uphill, with the Church on your left. You can visit the church and also enjoy the view over Bristol. On a clear day the Cotswold Hills can be seen, and to the left the Forest of Dean. Leave the churchyard by the gate opposite the Inn then turn left down the road. Approximately a quarter of a mile down the road you will come to a junction. Go over a stile at the side of a gate and continue in the same direction with the boundary on your left. At the end of this field, pass through a gate and carry on, still with the boundary on the left. Go over a stile, then a few yards further on go over another, and follow the path

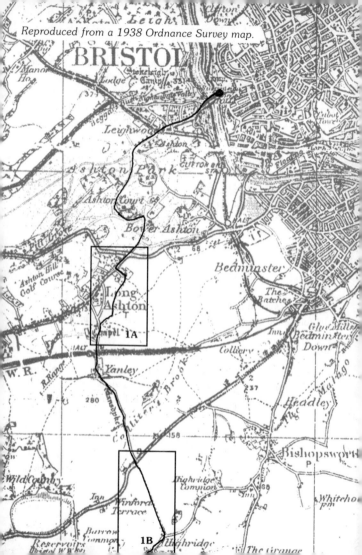

Reproduced from a 1938 Ordnance Survey map.

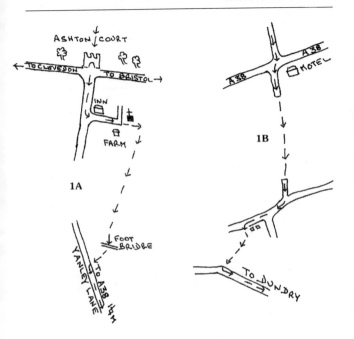

down a short way between a hedge and a communication station on the left, then over a stile. (Be careful of the concrete post above your head). Go straight ahead for a few hundred yards, across the corner of the field and cross over a stile.

You will come out into the open with an excellent view of the valley. Keep to the top of the field with the boundary on your left, then over a stile and on to a road. Turn right down the road (taking care), then after a few yards take the gate on the left and continue along the field in the same direction as before, following the left hand

11

Reproduced from a 1938 Ordnance Survey map.

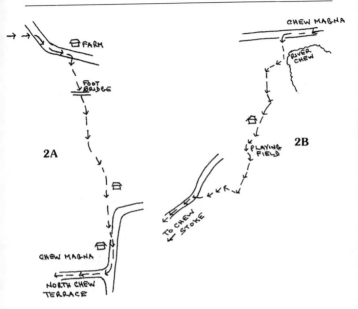

boundary, and over another stile. Go down this field with the boundary still on your left, cross a stile in the corner, down another field in the same direction, through a gate and over to a stile opposite, then turn right on a lane. Follow the lane down around a left-hand bend, and after a short way take a stile on the right, opposite a house. Follow the field down, keeping fairly close to the left-hand boundary, then go over a footbridge on the left. Turn right and continue close to the right hand boundary. At a corner, when you run out of boundary, cut over the field in the same direction, cross a stile then go up the next short field close to the right hand boundary to the stile opposite. In the next field, continue close to the left-hand boundary. Go over a stile at the side of a gate and carry on the same way, still close to the left-hand boundary. When the boundary runs out, cut straight over the field in the same direction to a well-concealed stile in the hedge. Drop down some steps into a field, then bear left down this small combe to a gate near the bottom corner. Once through the gate, continue down this long field, past a house on your left, to the very end. Go over a stile at the side of a gate, on a few yards to the stile opposite, down a few steps and on to a road. Turn right, continue for approximately 300 yards then take a road on your right "North Chew Terrace". You have arrived in Chew Magna.

A short distance on, with a stream on the left, bear left over an old stone bridge, arriving at St. Andrews's Church. Pass through the churchyard on to a major road. Turn right and continue past a couple of inns and some shops. Further up the road (approximately a quarter of a mile) are some staddlestones (or stone toadstools) on the left, where you turn left down a path. At the bottom of the path, do not cross the river, but turn right over a stile Go up the field and over another stile, then turn left and up through a small combe, and over a stile. Cross straight over the field towards a large oak tree, then over a stile. Bear right, with a house on the right, and cross over another stile near the wall. Then go ahead and over another stile, turn right and arc around a playing field. Keep on in the same direction as before the playing field, crossing a series of stiles. After the fourth one, bear right to the top of the field, over another stile, coming out on to a track. Turn left here, and follow the track around to the road, where you turn left. Soon you will arrive at a major junction (take care) where you go into Pilgrims Way, straight ahead. Continue down this minor road. Further on, the Yew Tree Inn is on your right. This is Chew Stoke. Should you decide to take a rest, you may find suitable accommodation in the area.

To continue, bear left at the Inn and carry on down the lane, passing the Rectory on your right. Going downhill, bear right on a lane called "The Street", over the bridge, then take School Lane to the right. Continue up the road, passing the school and other buildings. On a bend, cross over a stile on the left, heading for another stile opposite. As you continue up the fields, keeping fairly close to the left hand boundary, look back and see Chew Stoke with its church and, in the distance the slopes of Dundry.

A few yards further on, keeping to the right of a barn, you will have a view of the Chew Valley and its lake. Continue through the left-hand gate, then keeping close to the hedge on the right, pass through another gate and down the next long field. At the end, go through a gate and come on to a road. Turn right, and a little further on go past an obelisk and a farm on the right. Carry on up the road for a while. You are now on Breach Hill, a good habitat for wildflowers. Just before the power lines, cross the stile on your left, and another stile beyond. From here there are good views of the Chew Valley, and also the Mendip Hills.

Continue in the same direction, with the hedge on your left and some farm buildings on the right. Go over a stile, then through a gate on the left, arriving at a junction of footpaths. Keep to the track closest to the hedge on the right. Follow the track around until you reach a gate. Go through it, and a second one further on, then bear left down the middle of the field, crossing the stile opposite. Keep in the same direction over another stile, then continue down to the far

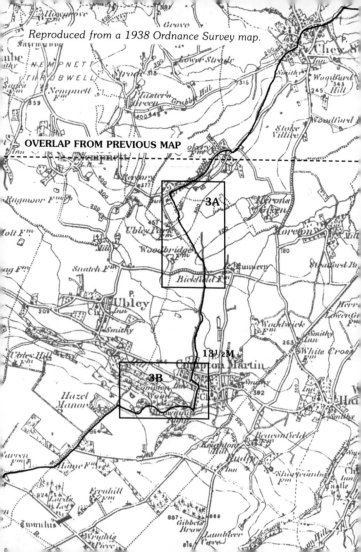

Reproduced from a 1938 Ordnance Survey map.

OVERLAP FROM PREVIOUS MAP

3A

3B

13 1/2 M

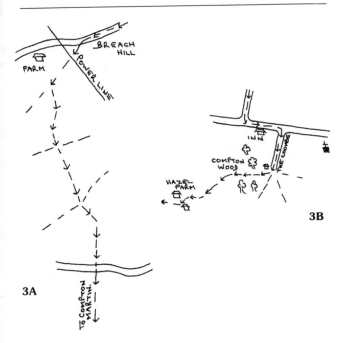

left-hand corner of the next field. Cross over a footbridge and stile, and carry on with the boundary on your left, and then go over a stile on to a road.

Walk straight over, then continue up the track opposite. Look out for the spindle bushes, whose presence probably indicates an ancient trackway. After about one mile you will reach the main road, then turn left into the village of Compton Martin, with the Ring o' Bells inn on your right. Just past the inn, turn right into a lane called

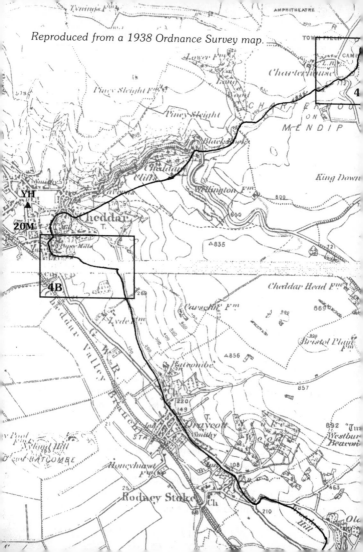

Reproduced from a 1938 Ordnance Survey map.

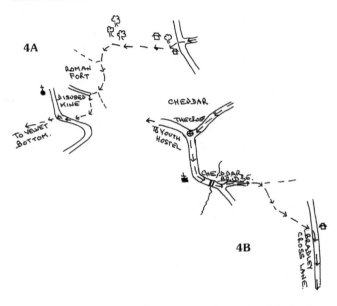

4A

ROMAN FORT

DISUSED MINE

TO VELVET BOTTOM.

CHEDDAR

THE CROSS

TO YOUTH HOSTEL

CHEDDAR BRIDGE.

4B

BRADLEY CROSS LANE.

The Coombe. Continue on up until you reach a series of footpaths and bridlepaths at the top. Follow the narrow path on the right near the building, which will take you on a long, steep climb through Compton Wood, coming into open ground at the top. Continue up the grassy slope on your left to a wall, pass through a gate, then go diagonally left through a gateway and farm buildings and bear right on a well-formed track. You are now on the Mendip Hills.

At the top of this farm track go over a cattle-grid, turn left and carry straight on through an avenue of beech trees, eventually passing a house on the right. Keep in the same direction until you reach a major road. Cross straight over and take the track opposite. A little further on, where the surfaced track swings right, take a short green track and go through a gate into a field. Follow the left-hand boundary and go over a stile into a Nature Reserve, eventually coming upon open ground where notices warning of disused shafts are displayed. Work your way around this area, along a gravel path, and bear left towards a car parking area. The track bears slightly right; a few yards further on go left through a gate. Follow the path to a road, turn right, and go up a few yards, then left and on to a well-defined track, entering another Conservation Area, and down to Velvet Bottom.

Continue down this delightful combe for approximately one mile, then go over two stone stiles, keeping to your left, and enter a National Trust area known as Black Rock. Eventually cross over the road and on to the footpath opposite. A very steep ascent will take you through woodlands and eventually into open country. Go through a gate, stay on the main path (avoid bearing left, but not too far right - there is a 500 foot drop). You will reach an escarpment with Cheddar Lake before you, Brent Knoll beyond, and below you Cheddar, one of the most popular villages in England.

To the right lies Cheddar Gorge, a natural habitat for the rare Cheddar Pink. To the far left, on a clear day, Glastonbury Tor can be seen, which will dominate the walk for a few days until you arrive in the Quantock Hills.

Descending the hill by a knobbly pathway, you will come to Jacob's ladder, which is a concessionary way. Its 237 steps will take you down into Cheddar Village, famous for its caves, cheese, cider and, in the right season, its strawberries, and cream teas. As an alternative to Jacob's Ladder, take the public right of way. Continue past the steps on your right, then bear slightly left. The path winds down to a lane. Turn right and walk approximately 100 yards, turn right again and go down another lane to a main road. Turn left, cross over the bridge, then bear left at a major junction into Cliff Street and follow the road for a quarter of a mile until you arrive at the Market Cross. There are plenty of shops here to replenish stocks.

(If going for the hostel, at the Cross, bear right into Bath Street, continue to a major junction and a war memorial, then turn right into a road called the Hayes. Carry on until you get to a lane on the left, Hillfield. The Hostel is up here).

CHEDDAR to BRIDGWATER: 29 MILES

Somerset Levels, Polden Hills and Villages

Leaving the cross in a southerly direction by Church Street, you will come to a church on your right. Continue for a few yards and then go over Cheddar Bridge (take care on this very dangerous bend). Once over the bridge, turn left on to a lane which, after a short distance dwindles into a footpath. At the top, enter a field and go up, keeping close to the right hand boundary, until you come to a stile on the right. Go over into a field, then cross to the opposite boundary and over another stile.

Cross two more fields, bearing slightly to your left, and going over two stone stiles. The second will bring you out into Bradley Cross Lane near a house.

Turn right and go along the lane for approximately one mile, arriving at the main road and the village of Draycott. This is quite a pleasant lane. It would have been better to have gone on the top of the Mendips and walked along the ridge, since here you finally leave these hills, but there is no direct footpath.

The next stage will take you over the Somerset levels. By looking through the hedge and gates, you get an idea of the sort of country through which you will be walking. On reaching Draycott, walk along the road for about one mile in the same direction to the next village of Rodney Stoke. Take great care; this is an extremely busy road, which seems short of footpaths. Along here you will find plenty of places to buy strawberries in the summer - produce seems to be everywhere. Carry on another half mile through the village, up the hill until you reach a signpost to Priddy. Take this small road on the left where there is some relief from the traffic, Perhaps one day there will be a top ridge path, which avoids the main road.

Go along the road for a short distance, then round a right hand bend. Continue up for approximately 300 yards, then just past a gate on the right go over a stile, head up the field to where it forms a small neck, and over another stile. Continue in a fairly straight line, going over a series of fields and stiles. On your right the scenery is more open. Glastonbury Tor can be seen in the distance., The small fields and meadows along here are delightful, and some very pleasant views surround them. Eventually, you will go over your last stile on this bearing - nearly all of them are made of fine Mendip stone - and you can see the village of Westbury-sub-Mendip. The path swings right; go down to the bottom of the field, where there is a stile which leads on to a lane. Turn left, then at the bottom of the lane turn right. Here you can see the Village Cross and the Church behind it. Accommo-dation should be available in the village. You are now on that busy road again, but thankfully not for long. Turn left; the Westbury Inn is on the left and soon after that on the right is Station Road. Go down here.

23

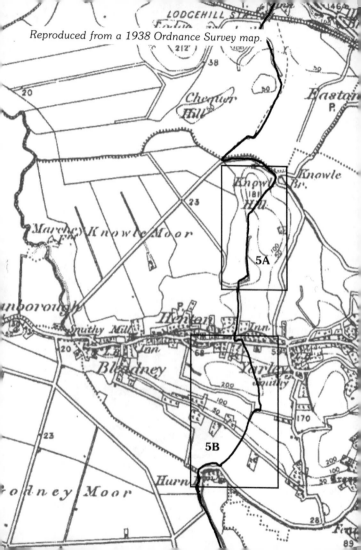

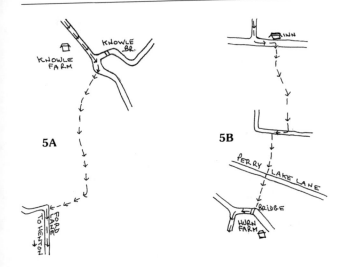

Continue over a bridge and a disused railway line, then turn left through some farm buildings. A few hundred yards further on turn left again at a junction. After another few hundred yards, ignore the turning on the left and carry on until the lane runs out. You will come to some gates. Take the one straight ahead. Follow the track around to the right and take a gate further on. Keeping fairly close to the right hand boundary, cross the next field over to a footbridge in the corner. Once over the footbridge, go through a gap on your right, turn left and walk down by the hedge. Go over another footbridge and continue down the next field with the rhyne on your left. At the end of this field, pass through a gate near the corner, turn right and follow the rhyne down on your right for approximately 300 yards until you are close to a line of trees. Then take a diagonal path off to the left across the field to another, larger, footbridge. Once over, you will find yourself on a road. Turn left and continue, passing a farm on the right, until you come to a bridge on the left. Don't cross it - bear right, go up here approximately 50 yards and then, on a bend, go through a gate on the right.

Walk up this field, keeping fairly close to the hedge on your left, and through another gate. Continue in roughly the same direction up the next field. Drop down the hill, where you will see a gate near the left-hand corner of the field. Go through this into a track between two hedges and continue on down, and eventually take a right hand turn. Go on along here for a short distance, arriving at Ford Lane. Turn left and walk straight to the main road; this is the village of Henton.

Turn left on the main road (take care). A short way down this road enter a field on the right, either by a stile or up a few steps a little further on. Walk to the top of the hill, heading for the far left-hand corner of the field. Go over a stile, then straight ahead for a short distance and cross the stile in the corner. Walk in the same direction, keeping the hedge on your left, go through a gate and come out on to a major track, and then turn right. A little way down you will come to a gate on your left, approximately 30 yards prior to a sharp right hand turn. Go through the gate and make your way to the bottom of the field, keeping reasonably close to the left-hand boundary. (At the bottom there should be a stile on to a lane and one opposite to take you in the same direction). If it is not there, turn right, keeping close to the boundary, and on to the corner). Go through a gate on to the lane, turn left, walk approximately 20 yards and take the second gate on the right, then go ahead bearing slightly to your left, to a gap in the hedge. In the next field, keep the rhyne on your left. You will then go through a gate near a stone bridge and come out

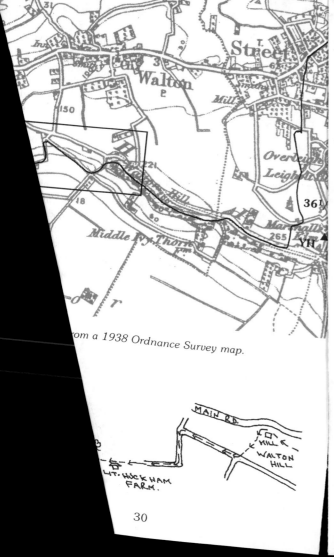

from a 1938 Ordnance Survey map.

on a road. Turn right. At the next junction bear left for Godney. A short way down here, go over a footbridge on the left, crossing the rhyne into the field.

Turn immediately right, go through a gate and continue along the field keeping close to the rhyne, which is on your right. Carrying on up here, go through two more gates, and eventually pass under some power lines. A little further on there is a footbridge on the right. Cross over, and then bear left, keeping close to the hedge on your left. At the end of the field go through a gate and on to the road. Do not turn left - go straight ahead. You are now coming to the village of Godney.

Turn left over the bridge, which is signposted to Glastonbury, pass Godney House on the left and continue along the road to Godney Farm. There are not many connecting rights of way over the levels, so it's going to be a bit of a trudge along the droves. However, there is an abundance of wildlife, sedges and willows, so make the most of it.

At Godney Farm the road bears left. As you carry straight on, the various plant life according to the season is worth noting. In early summer it is lined with yellow iris, patches of marsh marigold, and later purple loosestrife. You will go through an avenue of pollarded willows.

Continuing down, you will come to a bridge and a left-hand turn, which are approximately one and a half miles from Godney Farm. This is called Great Withy Drove. Go up here, then further on pass a stone bridge on the left. The road winds, and gives relief from the

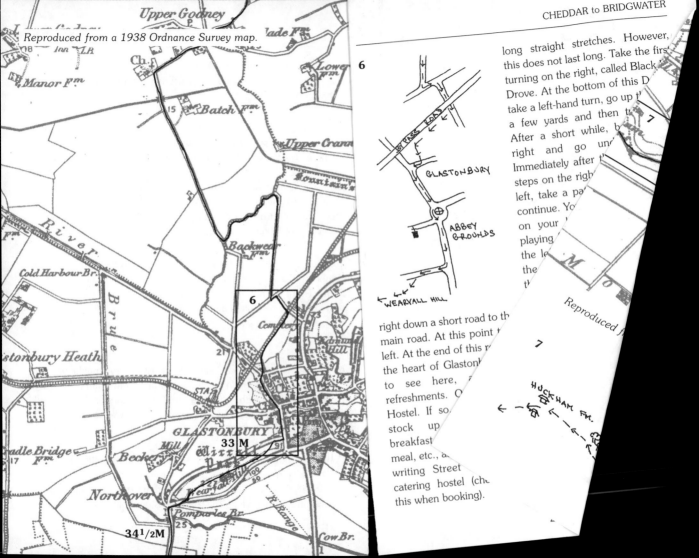

Reproduced from a 1938 Ordnance Survey map.

6

long straight stretches. However,
this does not last long. Take the firs
turning on the right, called Black
Drove. At the bottom of this D
take a left-hand turn, go up
a few yards and then t
After a short while, b
right and go un
Immediately after t
steps on the righ
left, take a pa
continue. Yo
on your
playing
the le
the
t

GLASTONBURY

ABBEY
GROUNDS

WEARYALL HILL

right down a short road to th
main road. At this point
left. At the end of this r
the heart of Glaston
to see here,
refreshments. O
Hostel. If so.
stock up
breakfast
meal, etc., a
writing Street
catering hostel (ch
this when booking).

HUCKHAM FM.

Reproduced f

7

To continue, bear right, along Market Place, take the Shepton Mallet road and go past the Abbey Gardens on the left. After a short while you will reach a roundabout. Turn right on the main road and go down here for about 400 yards. After the last house on the left there is a kissing gate; pass through it into the meadowland. Go diagonally right up Wearyall Hill, then walk along the ridge at the top. Look back; the Tor is quite impressive from here. Continue along this ridge, enjoying the distant views around you. As you descend, go over a stile. Street can be seen to the left, and the slopes of the Polden Hills, which you will be going along later. When you finally get to the end of this grassy ridge, pass through a stile in the left-hand corner, turn right on to the road and follow it down to the main road. Turn left, go across the River Brue up to the next major junction; at this point keep left and head for Street. A little further on there is another junction. Bear right here into High Street and the town centre. Continue up here, passing Clarks' Shoe Museum on the right. Carry on through the shopping centre, past the Crispin Hall, eventually coming to the Old Board School and a church on the right. Take the road opposite, and continue past a park on the right, and straight over into Oriel Road. At the end of this road there is Hecks Farmhouse Cider, Fine Cider Makers since 1840. Go straight ahead into Ivythorne Road. After a quarter of a mile the road bends to the left; at this point bear right up a road called Middle Brooks. A few hundred yards up this road, turn off on the left into Goose Lade. Go to the bottom of this short road, and turn right, and almost immediately left, and then over a stile into a field. Continue straight across the field to the far right hand corner, through a gap in the hedge then carry on up the footpath to the top of the next field, where you will go over a stile and into a lane. Turn right and walk down a couple of hundred yards, then a track on the left will go straight up to the Youth Hostel. (If you are not staying at the hostel, continue on the lane a little further, then a bridleway on the left will go up a hill, then turn right on a footpath which connects with the route from the Hostel).

If you stopped, leave the hostel on the opposite side to where you came in and turn immediately right. The walk has now changed direction - whereas you were coming south to this point, you are now heading west. Continue along this path; walking on a small ridge known as the Polden Hills. Go to the very end; the path will eventually run out and meet the road. Cross the road (take care) and join another path, continuing in the same direction. Eventually this path reaches a gate. Go through, and out into more open country. Up till now the views have been obstructed by growth. There is a viewpoint at the top of Walton Hill, which will give bearings to prominent landmarks. Continue in the same direction until you come to a converted windmill. Go past it on the right hand side and descend a slope, keeping close to the hedge on your left, then bear hard left around the mill, away from the road, and drop down to a stile in the right hand corner. This area of ground displays pyramidal orchids, thyme and rockrose in summer, with many species of butterfly amongst them. Go over the stile and drop down a few yards to a prominent track. Turn left, and continue descending between two hedges, coming to a minor road. Turn right and go uphill for approximately a quarter of a mile, then take a hard left hand turn on to a lane and drop down for a short distance. The lane will then swing right. Carry on and go over a stile at the side of a gate. On reaching the farm buildings, keep to the right of them and go through a gate into a field. Follow the left-hand boundary. A bit further on it will bend right. Continue uphill for a short way, then go over a well concealed stile on the left, into the trees. You will soon emerge into a meadow, another good wildflower habitat. Continue

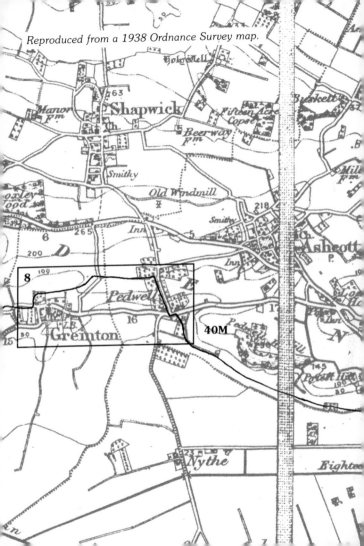

Reproduced from a 1938 Ordnance Survey map.

8

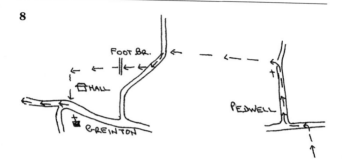

along the left hand boundary until you reach a gate on the left. Go through and carry on for a short distance, through another gate, up a grassy track, then drop down to another farm. Wind your way through the buildings (possibly waymarked) and you will find yourself on a well-formed track. Continue into a field. Keep the boundary on your right. At the end of the field go through a gate, under some power lines, to the gate opposite, back on a well defined track.

Further on, enter Redlands Farm. Pick your way through the buildings (possibly waymarked) and find yourself in a lane going in the same direction. Soon the lane bears around to the right, with an orchard on the left. At the end of the orchard, go over a footbridge into a paddock, cross the paddock to the gate opposite, then over the stile at the side of the gate and on to the road (take care). Turn left into the village of Pedwell, where there should be accommodation if required.

If you wish to carry on, go down the road about one hundred yards and then take a more minor road on the right called Pedwell Hill. Continue up here - the Methodist Church is on your left. 80 yards past the church, take the footpath on the left. Carry on, keeping to the right hand boundary, then pass through a gate into a field. Continue in a straight line, going over a stile near a dog-leg in the hedge, across a field and over a further stile, after which bear slightly to the left and through a gate on to a lane. Turn left, and after approximately 80 yards down the lane go over a stile on the right. This is fairly well concealed, so keep an eye open for it. Walk down this next field, keeping close to the hedge on the right, then go over a stile and footbridge and into the next field. Keep close to the left hand boundary and go through a gate, then bear left down to a neck in the field. Go through a gate in the corner, down a track, and you will find yourself on the main road again. This is the village of Greinton. Turn right on the road, which soon bears left, marked Taunton. Ignore this, and take the minor road straight ahead marked to Moorlynch. After a short while go round a left hand bend, then at a junction bear right and continue down the lane for half a mile towards Moorlynch.

Once in Moorlynch, if required, you may find accommodation. There is an inn called the Ring of Bells. The road takes a right hand swing up the hill, but you go straight ahead along the lane. You can take a well worthwhile diversion by continuing around the right hand bend up the hill for a quarter of a mile to visit the church, which is on your left. There are good views from the churchyard. On leaving the church to the south side, in the far right hand corner there is a gate into the field. Go through, follow the field down, keeping close to the left hand boundary, then over a stile and you will find yourself back on the original lane. Turn right and continue.

A little way along, a track goes off to the left. Ignore this, and keep to the top one. You are starting to climb a little, which will get you

Reproduced from a 1938 Ordnance Survey map.

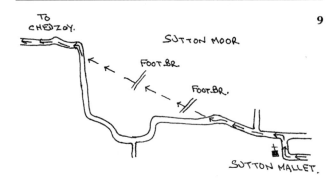

off the low country and give a better view. On a clear day the Quantocks can be seen, which you will be making for once through Bridgwater. This is a pleasant track, and you can make good progress, but it can be muddy at times. Carry on for a while. You will come across a bit of an elbow in the path; after this, keep going in the same direction. At the end of this track, (about one and a half miles from Moorlynch) is the village of Sutton Mallet. The track will lead on to a road. Go straight ahead to the church. Turn right, then after a short distance turn left on to the road marked "Chedzoy". Continue up here for about a quarter of a mile until you come to a left hand bend in the road. The next bit is a little tricky. You can make a choice here. On the bend, go into the field on your right. Walk up a little way and go over a footbridge on the right (head diagonally left towards the end of the ridge on your right) At this point you may need a compass bearing, heading north-westerly about 300 degrees.

However, if you are a little unsure about this, continue on the road; this will eventually turn right and arrive at the same point. If you

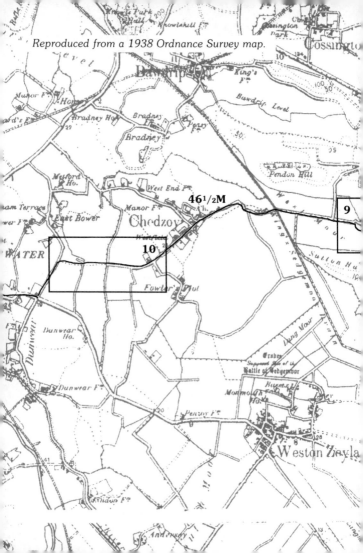

Reproduced from a 1938 Ordnance Survey map.

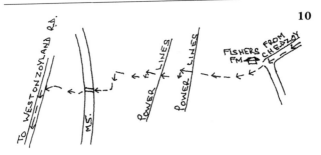

have taken a bearing, you will cross over another bridge. Continue on the same bearing; it will come to a rhyne. Officially the right of way goes over a bridge on the road. If this is missing, continue down for approximately 300 yards with the rhyne on your left, then come out on to the road and turn right. After a few yards the road bends left. You will soon come to a signpost to Stawell. Ignore this and carry on for half a mile to the Kings Sedgmoor Drain.

Once you cross the bridge over the drain, follow the winding little road for approximately three quarters of a mile to the village of Chedzoy. Be careful of the blind corners. The church is on your right; it is well worth a visit; the pews are especially fine. There is also a pub in the village if you require refreshment.

At the church, the road takes a left hand swing. Continue for about half a mile out of Chedzoy towards Weston Zoyland, then the road will turn left. Ignore this and take the track ahead. Passing Fishers Farm, continue along this track in a straight line. Go through a gateway, and carry straight on, not diverting. Soon you will go under a set of power lines. The path now takes a sharp left hand bend. Ignore this; go over the footbridge in front of you and then turn left into the field, walking at the side of the ditch, and then right. Follow the boundary. Go through a gap into the next field and follow the left hand boundary down in the same direction, passing under another set of power lines. At the end of this field, go over a stile on the left, then cross a footbridge to your right, and go straight ahead over the M5 footbridge.

Go over a small footbridge slightly to your right, into a field. Continue down the field, making for a stile in the left hand corner, on to a road. Turn left and make your way up to a major junction (on the A372, Westonzoyland road). Turn right and carry on along this road for approximately one mile. It will cross a railway line, then bend around to the right, meeting another road. You are very close to Bridgwater Railway Station, but don't catch the train home. There's a lot of beautiful country to come.

BRIDGWATER to LUXBOROUGH: 25 MILES

Quantock Hills, Brendon Villages and Hills

Coming off the Westonzoyland Road, you find yourself at a mini roundabout. Turn left into St. John Street. Continue for a few hundred yards to the first set of traffic lights, then turn left into Cranleigh Gardens. This arcs around to the right, with a park on your left. At the end of this short road you will come to a bridge crossing the River Parrett. Go over the bridge and continue to the next major junction. Turn left as if going to Barnstaple and North Devon. Immediately go over the road on a pedestrian crossing, then take a little lane on the left. Not far down here there is a bridge. Go over, turn left for a few yards, drop down to the water, turn sharp left again so that you are heading under the same bridge, then up the towpath with the canal on the right.

After a quarter of a mile the canal bends to the right; keep close to it, going under a bridge. A little further on there is another bridge, but don't go under this; take the slip lane up to the left which leads straight on to the main road. Then turn left. After approximately a hundred yards there is Westfield Church on the left. Still on your left hand side, you will see a playing field. Enter the field and cross over, heading slightly to the right, towards some allotments. Keep these on the left. At the end of the allotments, turn left and go down the path, with the hedge on your right, then over a stream. Turn right and go over a stile and follow the stream to the next boundary -

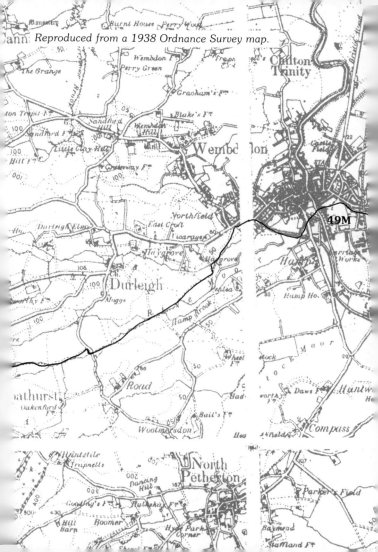

tarting to climb. If the weather is clear, look back and see
e country covered so far. The Mendip Hills are very plain,
ime to time you may see Glastonbury Tor, and also
Bay, which gives an idea of how you have gone round
w of Somerset.

his field, in the left hand corner, go through a gate.
me direction, close to the right hand boundary.
hrough another gate. Beyond that, just after the
ndary, there is quite a large oak on the right. At
he oak and take the gate on your right and walk
heading slightly right, and make for a bungalow.
galow, go through a gate and then turn left on
up here a short way and onto a minor road.
bit further on go over some crossroads as if
ogressing down here you will walk beneath
er, rose bay willow herb is in flower, and
tch and hawkbits. In spring early purple

approximately 200 yards - then head diagonally towards the left
hand corner of the field. Go over another stile, then follow the right
hand boundary down. At a bend in the path, just before an oak tree,
pass over a stile beside a gate on your right. Once in the field, head
diagonally left to another gate. Go through it, heading slightly left,
towards the opposite boundary. Well concealed in the hedge to the
right of an ash tree is an iron stile and a footbridge. Cross over,
follow the next field down, keeping close to the right hand boundary.
In the corner you will find a stile. Once over this, go over a
footbridge to the left, then down the next small field. Following the
right hand boundary again, go over another stile. At the end of this
field, ignore the gate and turn left, keeping the boundary on your
right. After approximately 100 yards, cross another footbridge
directly underneath some power lines on the right. Turn left down
the next field for a short way, keeping close to the left hand
boundary. After approximately 250 yards, cross over a footbridge
on the left. Continue down (it's quite a long field), keeping close to
the right hand boundary. In the far bottom right hand corner go over
another footbridge on the right and enter a small field. Follow the
left hand boundary down and then go through a gate in the right
hand corner and onto a road.

This can be quite an exhausting stretch from Bridgwater Station
as regards map reading, the footbridges and stiles are well
concealed.

Turn right on the road, go round the bend, and there is a footpath
on your left. Go through the gate into the field. Head towards the
prominent pylon, until you reach the field boundary, then walk down
the same field, with the boundary on the left. You will go under more
power lines, but there are compensations for their lack of charm; if

Reproduced from a 1938 Ordnance Survey map.

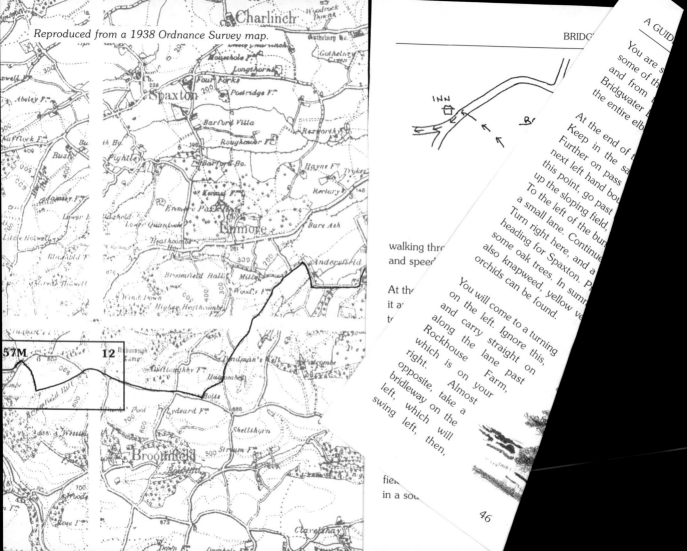

You are s
some of th
and from
Bridgwater
the entire elb

At the end of
Keep in the sa
Further on pass
next left hand bo
this point, go past
up the sloping field.
To the left of the bu
a small lane. Continue
Turn right here, and a
heading for Spaxton. P
some oak trees. In summ
also knapweed, yellow ve
orchids can be found.

walking thr
and speed

At th
it a
t

You will come to a turning
on the left. Ignore this,
and carry straight on
along the lane past
Rockhouse Farm,
which is on your
right. Almost
opposite, take a
bridleway on the
left, which will
swing left, then,

fiel
in a sou

the track divides. Follow the right hand track and continue for approximately half a mile, keeping close to the right hand boundary.

At a junction of paths turn right, go over a stile into a National Trust area marked Broomfield Hill. Notice the view to the left before following the path down over a couple of stiles, then cross over a busy main road (take care), then turn left to the Traveller's Rest Inn. Just past the inn is a small lane on the right. Go down here; towards the bottom of the combe you will see Manor Farm on the right and Waterpits Farm on the left (where accommodation may be found).

Up a slope, the lane comes out on to a road. Go straight over, and at the right hand side of Timbercombe Lodge a bridleway will take you on in the same direction. Continue along here for some distance, not diverting or going through any gates. The path will then start to enter a wood and go uphill. Eventually there is a junction of various paths. Ignore the wide one hard right. The one you want is a small track a few yards further on. The broad track on the left of this is a forestry or farm track. If you happen to take it by mistake and end up on the road, just turn to the right, go straight ahead and you will end up at the same point.

If you did manage to keep on the correct path, it will end up at the junction of roads and paths called Park End.

Now take the road on the right marked to Bagborough and travel uphill in a north-westerly direction. Half a mile up this road you will come to a junction. Don't turn left for Minehead; go straight on (marked for the car park). The lane gives a good display of foxgloves and tormentil in summer. (To avoid the narrow lane, there is a permissive bridleway to the right).

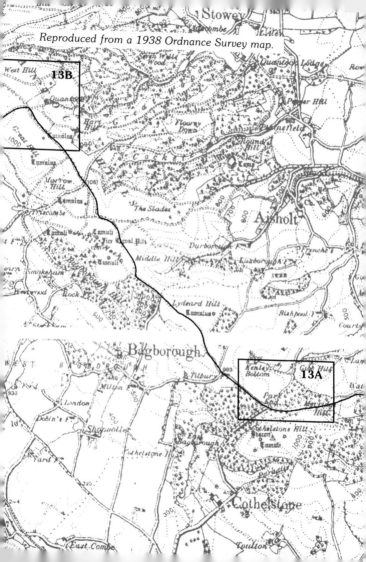

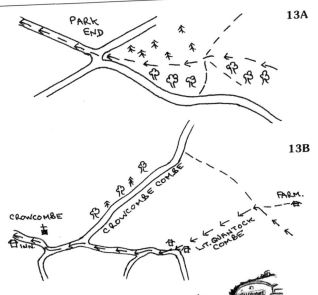

Arriving at the car park, cross over to the opposite side and still going in a north-westerly direction take the track straight ahead. This is the top of the Quantocks; the views are quite spectacular to the left. Carry on along this track with gorse on the right; you then come to a line of beech trees on your left. Continue straight ahead, and notice the abundance of ferns growing here.

Further on there is a gate and a stile. Go through and continue in the same direction.

Proceed along this track, still with beech trees on the left. At the end of the beeches, the path forks; take the path to the right. In late August or beginning of September, there are various heathers in bloom, with bees hard at work collecting the pollen.

Carry on; you will see a wood ahead. Continue along the track; it will take a right hand swing, but take the path slightly to the left, towards the corner of the wood. Then cut down the side, beneath a canopy of beech trees. The path bends off to the right a little - there are pine trees to your right and fairly open scrub ground to the left. You can make very good progress along this well defined track. At no time lose contact with the open ground on the left, even though it may be scrub.

Eventually you will come to another car park, which is through a gate on the right, but carry straight on through the beech trees until you come to a gate. Go through it and continue in the same direction. Further on there is another gateway; pass through it and carry straight on for approximately one third of a mile. Go through a hunting gate on your left. Once through the gate there is a pond; then head straight down the combe, following a long line of beeches on the right. This is known as Little Quantock Combe. (If you happen to have missed this gate and carried on, don't worry too much about it; you will come to a road - go left on the road known as Crowcombe Combe and you should end up in the village.)

Now hopefully you've come down Little Quantock Combe at the bottom of which there is a small farmyard. Pass through two gates on to a lane, then turn right. Past the first bend in the road, another lane goes off to the left; ignore this and take the one straight ahead. These lanes are a picture in the spring, but it seems the tops of the

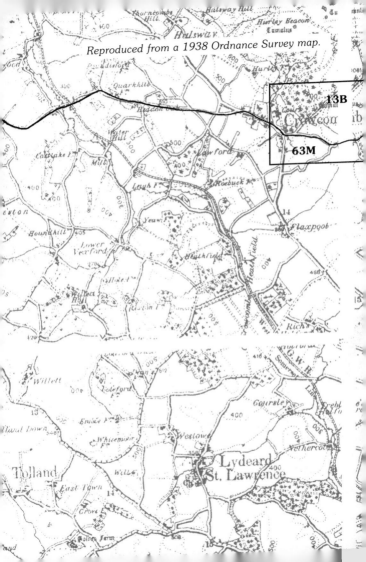

Reproduced from a 1938 Ordnance Survey map.

13B

63M

hills can match this during the summer. The road gradually winds its way down to a junction. At this point bear left (marked to Taunton). A few yards down the road you will find yourself in the village of Crowcombe. At a junction of roads, turn right as if going to Stogumber. On the right you have the village church and, on the left, one of the finest church houses in England. Carry on a little further with the cross on your right, and on the left the Carew Arms. Accommodation may be found here.

There will be quite a bit of lane walking for the next few miles. This is because there is no direct footpath. Anyway, it would be a great shame to miss the Somerset villages. Continue up the road for a quarter of a mile. The road then takes a sharp left hand swing down to a main road. Cross straight over this busy road into the lane opposite, signposted 'Stogumber'. You are walking on this lane right through to Stogumber - about two and a half miles - so keep straight ahead, not diverting off on any side lane. In August there is ribwort plaintain, sorrel, plenty of hips, blackberries and the red berries of

Wild Arum which shine like small lamps. Earlier the dog-roses are in bloom, mingling with honeysuckle, foxgloves and campion.

After a while the lane starts to drop down as you go under some quite large oak and beech trees, with a view of the Quantock Ridge to the right. At a crossroads; go straight on, past Quarkhill Farm on the right.

A bit further on, pass Brewers Water Farm on the right, and as you go down the hill the countryside of the Brendon Hills stretches out in front.

At the bottom of the hill, there is the West Somerset Steam Railway and Stogumber Station. Go under the railway bridge. On the left just past this you have the Bee World and Animal Centre. Pass over the stream and under the power lines. Continue straight over the next small crossroads. As you carry on, the road starts to go uphill. You will reach Stogumber Cricket Field on the right, with a quarter of a mile to go to the village centre. Just after a school, you will find Hall Farm on the right.

Continue down the road, which bends to the right. Go straight on for the village and church, but for the main route take a slip road on the left, then turn right at the bottom. Walk a short way, then turn left on the road and go straight on up the hill past a thatched house on the left. There will be a lane on the right marked 'Monksilver'. Ignore this and carry on up the hill. You are going to Monksilver, but the main reason to chose this route is that if you continue up the hill, taking the next turning on the right marked 'Combe Cross Lane' you will get better views. As you walk along this lane, look to your right and see Stogumber village and the church, with the Quantocks in the

background. You are then boxed in a bit by the hedges, but there are gateways to admire the view.

Approaching the top of the hill, the higher road does seem to have been worthwhile. In summer there is yellow toadflax on the side of the lane before you start to drop down. You now come to Combe Cross itself, a junction of lanes. Turn right on the road marked 'Monksilver. Immediately go to the left, past a thatched cottage. A short distance up the road, turn right at the signpost to Monksilver. You drop down quite steeply now, and can see Monksilver and its church on the left, and quite possibly deer on Birds Hill to your left. At Monksilver you will be at the end of the lane walking for the time being. From now on you will walk mostly on track, footpath and bridleway.

This is the heart of the Brendon Hills and their villages. Approaching Monksilver, the Community Hall will be on the right. Walk down the lane beneath some large oak trees. The lane swings left on to another road. Turn

Reproduced from a 1938 Ordnance Survey map.

right and go over a bridge. Once over the stream, ignore the turning on the right and continue for a few yards along the main road. The road swings right and you will see the Notley Arms ahead, where there may be accommodation. On this bend, take the lane to the left, then after about 50 yards follow a bridleway on your left to Colton Cross. This is a wonderful little combe. A few years ago it was a running stream, but a lot of work has been done on the path since then. It is quite hard coming up here, but to compensate the sides are covered in harts tongue fern, lichens, mosses and liverworts.

After some distance the path starts to level out. At the beginning of June there were still lesser celandines in flower. You may find cones on the ground beneath a couple of Scots pines, but the trees are mainly oak, with holly and elder beneath. In August you can hear the drum of harvesters moving across the fields below. If the fields have been freshly ploughed and harrowed, they stand out like red carpets.

Carry on climbing up here for about one and a half miles. The path is well way-marked, well maintained and a naturalist's haven. Eventually you will reach some beech trees, with a sign to Monksilver. There is a track to the left. Don't take

Reproduced from a 1938 Ordnance Survey map.

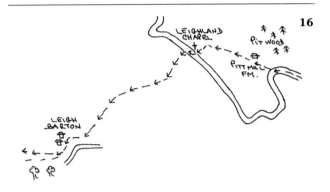

that - just carry straight on to more open ground with bracken on the left and woodland on the right.

At the end of this track there is a gate and a junction of lanes. Cross straight over - not the one to Holcombe Farm, nor the one on the right that goes down the hill - just go straight on.

About a quarter of a mile up this lane turn right at a footpath sign. Go through a gate and into a field. Once through the gate, keeping to the narrow part of the field, go straight over to the wood. In the corner, go through a gate. Once through, there are several tracks ahead. The one on your left is a forestry track. You want the one that goes ahead, and drops down the hill. It should be waymarked on the first oak tree on the right. You will soon know if you are on the right track. Although you are walking in the wood, immediately to the right there is open ground. This is a good ridge. You are now walking under beech trees, and looking down the valley to the right you can see the hamlet of Chidgley below. The track swings gradually to the left, descending all the time. You will soon come to a junction of paths, one marked Raleigh's Cross. Ignore this and go straight downhill. You will then come to a main road. Turn immediately right and continue down the hill. Notice an old milestone on your left, saying 5 miles to Watchet. You will not be on this road for long, but it can be very busy, so take care. On the left is a lane that doubles back on you - take this one. Carry on down the lane, which takes a right hand turn past Willhay Farm on the right (it can be quite slippery down here when wet) and continues, going down quite steeply.

Eventually pass through a small tunnel, and shortly after that there is a waterfall on the left. Carry on for a short distance; the track will suddenly swing hard to the left. At this point there is Pitt Farm on the right. Go up the farm track for about 60 yards, then on your left you will see a hunting gate. Go through this and continue. You will find yourself in a small field. Keep to the top of this field, close to the boundary, which will be on the left. On the opposite bank is Pit Wood, which is mostly conifers. At the other end of the field you will come to some steps, and a stile. Go over it and continue up the path between two banks. This path does not go on for long. It will swing hard to the right. At this point, pass through the small gate on your left into the churchyard. Once through the churchyard, go through another gate and on to the lane. This is the village of Leighland Chapel. Turn right on to the lane and walk up it for about 20 yards, then take the footpath on the left. Walk up a look over the gate on your right at the view. Immediately to your right there is the Quantock ridge, gradually fading away. On the left you can see Exmoor looming up, which will now dominate the route. Continue down; until the lane starts to turn left, on your right are two gateways and a signpost, which says "Footpath to Luxborough". Go through the gate into the field and walk in the direction indicated by the signpost - don't take the path to Roadwater.

Once in the field, keep parallel to the left hand boundary, over to a line of beech trees. Go through a gap in the trees; walk on a little further and go through a gate on the left hand side. Once through the gate, take a diagonal route over the field in a north-westerly direction. Follow the field to the bottom left hand corner, to the right some oaks.

On the opposite hillside there is Slowly Wood, and Slowly Farm buildings. Arriving at the bottom of the field, pass through the furthest gate in the corner. Once through here, you will find yourself in a long field; bear to the left and continue to go up the whole length of this field, keeping close to the left hand boundary.

At the other end of the field, go over the stile near the gate on the far right, then bear very slightly to your right, walk down a

short way and you will come to a gate. Go through the gate and across the next field (keeping close to the left hand boundary) to the gate opposite. Once through the gate, turn right, then go immediately through another gate, continue in the same direction as the last field, and straight across the field at its narrowest point. It is a bit steep coming up here. After a short distance you will come to a hunting gate. Go through it and continue roughly in the same direction, keeping close to the left hand boundary. You are still going uphill, but are getting the reward for your effort.

You are now in open country. Keeping fairly close to the left hand boundary, you will come to a gate, but don't go through it. You are at the top of the hill here, have a sit down and look at the view. Then continue down the boundary of the same field, which is still on the left. At the corner is a stile. Go over it, and straight ahead on a well-formed track. Take the second gate on the right, and enter a copse, with a pond on the right. Walk straight up the track and pass through the next gate, then turn left and up another track. Follow this round for a short way and you will come to a farmyard. In the middle of the farmyard there should be a signpost. One track is marked to Combe Berrow, half a mile. Do not take this one. Take the one to Raleigh's Cross. Immediately past this point, still in the farmyard, the track splits again. Take the route uphill and walk straight ahead, keeping the hedge on your right. Very soon there will be another gate. Pass through it and you will find yourself in open country with a deep valley on the left. On the other side of the valley there is Forehill Wood. Continue straight ahead on a steady climb. This can be ablaze with colour in summer, with foxgloves, plenty of brambles still in flower, thistledown and a certain amount of gorse. There are grasshoppers and meadow brown butterflies, and the place can be alive with rabbits. At the top of this ridge, go through a gate and on to another path between two hedges, then you will

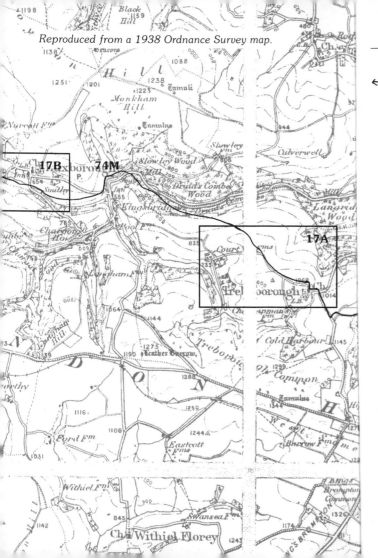

Reproduced from a 1938 Ordnance Survey map.

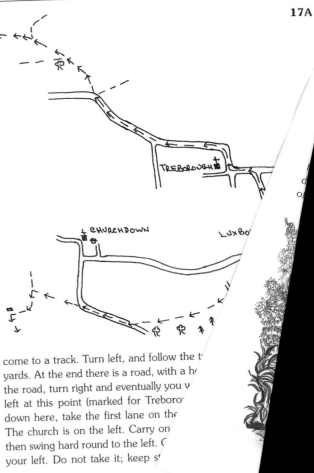

come to a track. Turn left, and follow the t
yards. At the end there is a road, with a h
the road, turn right and eventually you v
left at this point (marked for Treboro
down here, take the first lane on the
The church is on the left. Carry on
then swing hard round to the left. C
your left. Do not take it; keep s

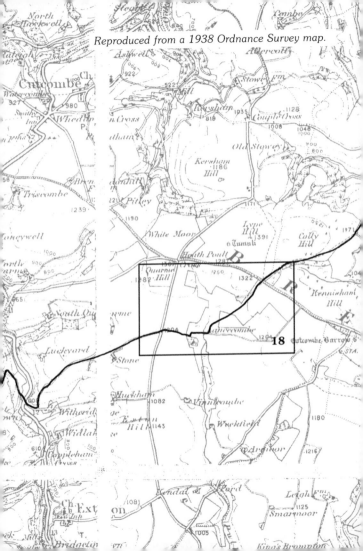

Reproduced from a 1938 Ordnance Survey map.

18

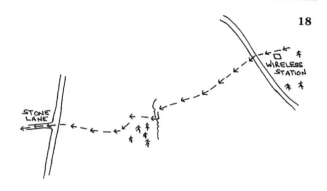

18

slope, meeting another major track, and continue in roughly the same direction between tall pines. The track eventually swings round to the left down to a road. Bear left. The Washford River is on your right, carry on a little further on. Ignore the road to the right to Rodhuish and go straight on. You may see a water vole and dippers in the river, and mimulus or monkey flower grows near a bridge. This is the village of Luxborough. There should be accommodation. There is an inn - the Royal Oak, or more accommodation may be found a bit further along the route at Churchdown.

LUXBOROUGH to LYNTON: 26 MILES

EXMOOR, DOONE VALLEY AND THE CLEAVES

The next stage will cover the Exmoor National Park, still a land of villages, with a lot more moorland and rivers in the second half. After crossing the bridge in Luxborough go up the road towards Dunster, passing the Royal Oak on your right. Just past the Inn, take a footpath on the left. A little further on, go over a stile, and then enter a field, keeping to the left-hand boundary. After a few hundred yards, go over a footbridge on the left, then turn right and carry on with the water on your right. Walk down here past a house. Keep right and close to the water. A little further there is a road; continue in the same direction. The road goes downhill and swings to the right. At this point, if you are going to Churchdown keep to the road. If not, take the footpath on the left, go over the stile, then straight ahead to the opposite boundary and over another stile. Follow the right hand boundary and go through a gate, then turn left on a well defined track. Continue a little way; the track swings to the right; follow it uphill for a short distance, then pass through a gate on the left and into a field. Continue up the field (it is very steep here), keeping close to the right hand boundary. Look down the valley to the area that you have just covered, with Churchdown on the opposite side. Go through the gate at the top of the field. You will be climbing a slippery, stone-based track between beech hedges. Then come out into the open. Carry on in the same direction up the track.

You will still be going up a hill, but not quite so steeply. As you walk on, there are a couple of gates ahead; take the first gate on the right. Just beyond this, the path splits. There is a signpost here to Wheddon Cross, ignore this. Go more or less straight ahead, keeping close to the left hand boundary (the signpost you follow will say Luxborough, Chargot).

Keep following the left hand boundary through two further gates, then pass through a hunting gate and follow the same boundary down approximately 200 yards and go through a gate on the left. Turn right, heading in the same direction up a short track and through a barrier . At this point there is a wireless station on your immediate left. Continue on the track until you reach the main road. Turn right, then almost immediately left through a gate and walk down the field through another two gates, keeping parallel to the right hand boundary. Coming down here and looking slightly to the left, you can see the moor you will be crossing. At the moment, the nearest stop is Winsford.

Once through the second gate, go over slightly to the right so that you meet the right hand boundary corner, where you pass through a gate into another field. Keep more or less on the same bearing, crossing diagonally to the very far corner. You should be heading towards a large clump of beech trees. On the right, in the very corner of the field, go through a gate and over a stream. After crossing the stream, walk straight ahead for approximately 200 yards, keeping parallel with the left hand field boundary, then head for the last large beech tree on the left. At this point, come in close to the left hand boundary and continue up the field. Pass through a gate and carry on in the same direction. At the end of this field there is another gate to go through, and you will find yourself on a road. Opposite there is a lane; walk straight down. Before doing so, look through a gate on your right. Weather permitting, Dunkery Beacon stands out quite plainly.

The lane continues for a good mile. As you carry on, it starts to drop down. There are some beech trees on the left and the lane then swings around a little bit. Stone Farm is on the left. This is an excellent lane to wander down. You can see all the country spread out in front of you, giving an idea of where you are going, and at the same time allowing you a rest from opening and closing gates, going over stiles and looking at the map. Continuing down, you reach a hard right hand swing in the lane, and a short while later a main road. Cross straight over the road on to the track opposite. A few yards down here, you will come to a stream and cross a footbridge. Once over, take the track to the right, going uphill. and continue under a canopy of various growth. When you reach a gate, go through and carry on the same way. The base of the track is rock, and slippery when wet.

Towards the end of the track there is a very hard left hand turn. Continue on to the top of the hill, with open ground on the left. Here is a good opportunity to rest.

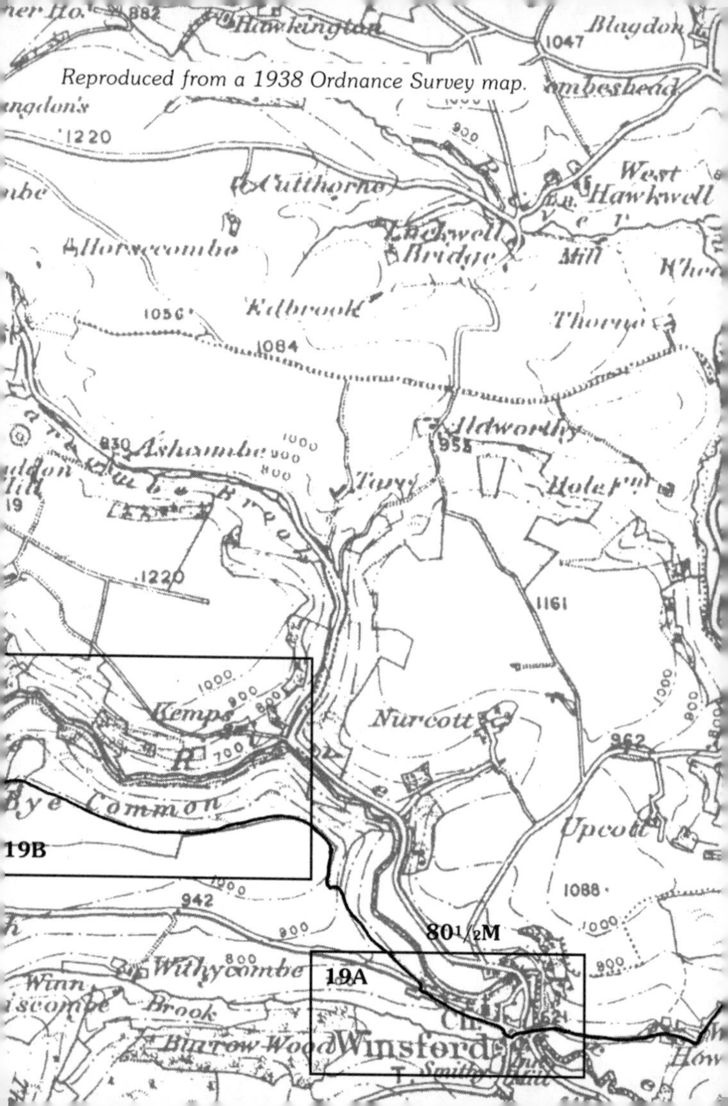

Reproduced from a 1938 Ordnance Survey map.

19B

19A

80½M

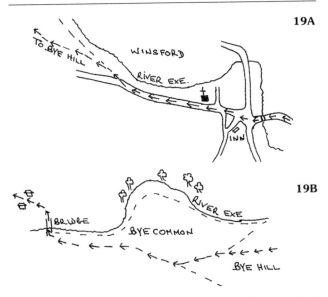

Walk on in the same direction - the path takes a slight right hand turn. You will come to a gate; go through it and continue straight on between two hedges, not diverting off this track at all. It will soon start to go downhill, with a sharp right hand turn at the end, taking you into a lane. The lane carries on for about half a mile, past a cricket field on the left.

You are now approaching Winsford, where accommodation may be found. With the lane levelling out now, and the hedge a bit lower, you can see Winsford Church. Pass over a bridge - underneath is the River Exe, which dominates this part of the walk. At the end of the lane, go straight over the road and continue, with the village cross on the left, and also the Royal Oak inn, a beautiful thatched building. Continue towards the church. (If you want to see the church take the first lane on your right. Orange hawkweed, or fox and cubs, flowers in the churchyard during July and August). Otherwise proceed with houses on either side. Ignore the footpath sign on your left, and continue for a further 60 yards to a gate and footpath sign on the right. Once through the gate, another 60 yards down the track, the path splits again. As an alternative, you can take the track on the right and more or less follow the river all the way to Exford, but the main route goes to the left via Bye Common. This means quite a climb for half a mile but it is well worth it for the views at the top. The path drops down to the river a bit further on, so this way you can have the best of both worlds. Carry on up here, and after a short distance go through a hunting gate. Keep close to the left hand boundary. Look back at the view as you climb. Further on, pass through another hunting gate and immediately turn left. After a steep climb for a few yards, turn right into a field and walk in the same direction as before. There are magnificent views at the top. Levelling out now, with trees on the right and a field on the left, you come to two large beech trees. Go through two hunting gates, one straight ahead and then one immediately on the right. After the second, turn left amongst bracken. Continue along this ridge - you will find the climb has been well worth it.

Eventually pass through another hunting gate. Further on, drop down to a more major track, keeping in the same direction. Continue on through a gate and then go up a small slope and into a long field. Go along the field in a westerly direction making for a footpath sign, then start to bear right and drop down. You will descend fairly rapidly now, but carry on more or less in the same direction, through a gate and keep to the right hand boundary, then take the next gate on the right. Continue in the same direction, keeping close to the left hand boundary now. In front, or slightly to the right, there is a row of beech trees. Go through another gate and continue on a well-formed track, descending very quickly now down to the River Exe. On reaching the bottom of the track you will meet another track at the side of the river. Carry on in the same direction for a short way and cross the bridge on your right. Once across, continue straight on, then bear left on the track.

Continue, and go through some farm buildings known as East Nethercott. Once through the farm buildings, a track comes down from the right. Ignore it, and go straight on through a gate, across a stream and up to some more buildings. Don't go down to the house. Turn to the right a little and cut in between the farm buildings. Go through a gate, then bear right following the track through a series of gateways. Beyond this, it appears as though the path splits, but keep in a straight line and to the top track, the one slightly to the right. Follow this pleasant little path, with no more gates for a while. Eventually it will come out into the open. Carry on, then you will start to swing around to the right, through gorse and silver birch trees. Continue down the path, eventually going through a couple of gates. As you drop down to the next gate, notice the old stone bridge on the left. Once through this gate you will come to a junction, but walk straight on. Go between buildings known as Lyncombe. Once through the buildings pass through a gate. The track appears to go straight on, but don't take this; take the gate on your left, then turn right, keeping fairly close to the right hand boundary. It should be quite well waymarked here.

After approximately 100 yards the path bends to the left, straight across the field. It can be quite boggy here. Enter a small neck of the

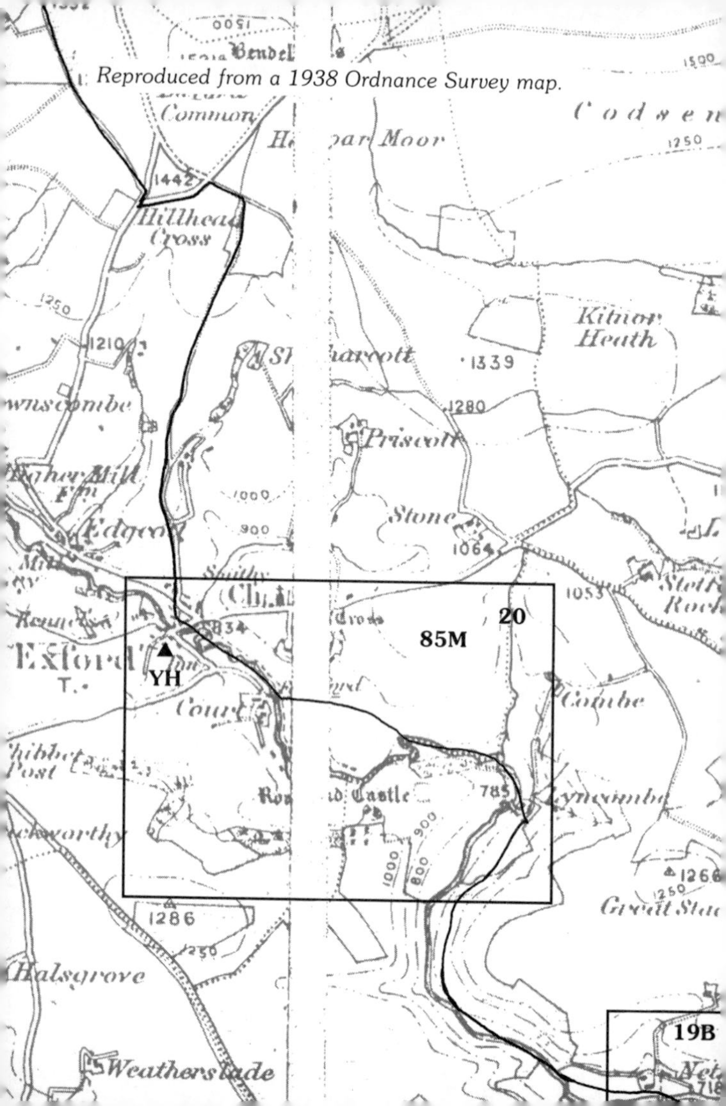

Reproduced from a 1938 Ordnance Survey map.

Codsen

Hepar Moor

Common

1500

1250

1442

Hillhead
Cross

Kitnor
Heath

1250

1210

Sharcott

·1339

wnscombe

1280

Priscott

Roher Mill
Fm

1000

900

Edger

Stone
1064

Smith

Chi

1053

Sleth
Rock

834

Grove

20

85M

Exford
T.

YH

Combe

Court

785

Lyncombe

hibbet
Post

Rod Castle

1000

900

ckworthy

800

1266

1250

Great Sta

1286

1250

Halsgrove

19B

Weatherstade

Ne

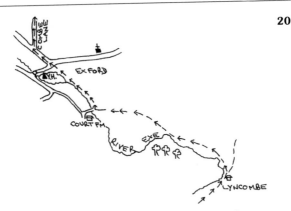

field, keeping close to the right hand boundary. You will not go very far before you cross over a stile, then over a footbridge and a further stile. Have a rest here; you may see a kingfisher.

To move on - go straight over another stile into the field. Keep reasonably close to the river. The path swings to the right, and in the corner cross a small stream. Once over, carry on straight ahead, keeping close to the right hand boundary. At the end of the field, pass through a gate and continue on the footpath. It goes across the field, taking a right hand sweep into the corner. Go over the stile, swing round to the left and straight down the track, keeping close to the boundary on your right. At the end of this path, before the bridge, go through a gate on the right. Follow the river and go through another gate, then on a bit through a further gate into a car parking area and on to the road. You are at Exford, and in the heart of Exmoor. There is plenty of accommodation and food here, shops to stock up and a couple of pubs. To get to the Youth Hostel, turn left, cross the bridge, bear left and left again. To continue on the main route, take the Porlock road, passing the Post Office on the right, and approximately 50 yards further on go up Combe Lane on your right.

The lane is fairly steep. Continue up here for approximately one mile, not diverting. There are tall hedges on either side. Eventually you will pass through a gate. There is now open ground on the left, with a beech hedge on the right. Go straight ahead through another gate. At the end of the next field there are a pair of gates. Ignore the one straight ahead and take the one on the right. Immediately turn left and continue along a bridle path. The country is open here, and to the right is Dunkery Beacon. At the end of this field, pass through a gate and immediately turn left on to a track. This does not go very far, before reaching a road. Turn left on the road (marked to Exford) and continue down here for a quarter of a mile. Eventually it will meet another road. Turn right on this one, walk up here for a few yards, and round a bend, then take the lane off to the left. It should be signposted to Alderman's Barrow. Carry on down here for two thirds of a mile. It is rather enclosed by beech hedges. After approximately half a mile, the view opens out a little and you can see the moor in front, then the lane comes to an end. Continue in the same direction on a well formed track.

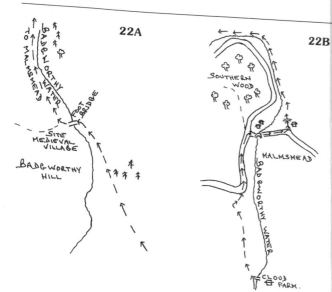

22A

22B

Reproduced from a 1938 Ordnance Survey map.

and there will be a footbridge below. Cross the footbridge, then go through a gate. Once through the gate, turn right and follow the path As you go on downstream there are gentle hills on each side, covered with heather, and numerous rowan trees. You are now in Devon.

Further on, the path suddenly takes a left-hand turn and after a short distance it will cross another footbridge. On the other side, pass through a gate. There will be a signpost and a "crossroads" of paths. Go straight over, up the slope (signposted Malmsmead). After a short distance, turn right and continue down the river. You are now walking down the valley at a slightly higher level, with the river on

When the track ends, go through a gate, immediately turn left, keeping close to the left hand boundary. Continue in this general direction for approximately one mile, and you will reach a minor road. Go straight over and through a hunting gate. You are now travelling in a north-westerly direction into open moorland. There is no boundary to follow, and in bad weather the use of a compass is advisable, but the track is fairly well defined and you continue in the same direction. After a while the path starts to bend to the left a little and eventually it will come to a gate. Once through, turn right and walk down the track for about 100 yards, then through another gate. Turn immediately left and follow the track down with the fence on your left.

There will be some beech trees on the right at the aptly named Larkbarrow. Skylarks are in abundance here. Go through two gates, and at this point you have covered 90 miles from Bristol.

Continue on the well defined path. It will reach a signpost and a gate. Pass through the gate and straight on. There is a line of beech trees on the right and then open moor on the left. Continue for a little way, reaching a gate and a signpost. Once through the gate, walk straight on towards the Doone Valley. There is a vast expanse of moorland in front of you, but you won't be crossing it. Further on, the track starts to bend to the right, and it comes to a hunting gate. Before you go through it, stop and look all around at a continuous horizon without road or car in sight.

When through the hunting gate, take a bearing slightly to the left, and follow the track down to the valley. At the bottom of a slope, go over a stream and then climb the slope at the other side. Proceed along the track, away from the water, then drop down a rocky path

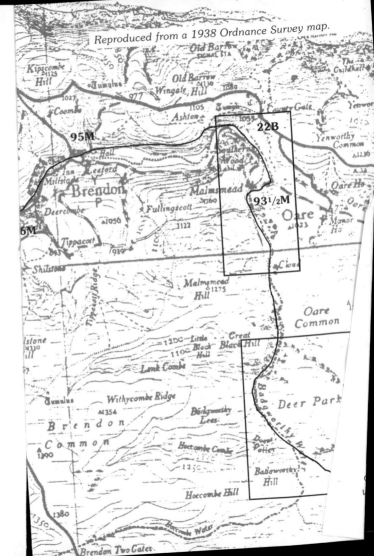

Reproduced from a 1938 Ordnance Survey map.

your right. You may see some dippers. Drop down into some woodland. Cross a stream, turn right a bit, then the track goes down a rocky path, close to the water again. You now continue on a level path. Further on, there will be a few tall pines on your right, and the path will go through rhododendron bushes and oaks. As you come into the oaks, cross over another footbridge on the left and continue in the same direction. You will eventually pass through another gate, when coming out of the oaks into the open. Carry on for a while, then dropping down the track you will see a footbridge on your right, going over the river to Cloud Farm, where you may get a cup of tea. Otherwise continue on, bearing to the left up to a gate, pass through the gate and go straight ahead on the track. You have now come away from the water, on a sort of ridge with very pleasant views. Continue for a while. The track then swings to the left and back on itself in a sort of "dog-leg". A little further on, it goes through a gate and on to a road. Go straight ahead in the same direction down to a junction. This is Malmsmead, where more refreshments are available. At the junction, turn right and go over the bridge. Follow the road straight ahead; for a brief moment you are back in Somerset. Continue along the road for approximately a quarter of a mile. On a right hand bend take a path which goes off to the left, passing through a gateway. Follow on past a house on the right, through a gate, then drop down and go over a footbridge. Turn left, with the water on your left and a hillside of gorse on the right. Further on, go through a gate. Keep close to the river, going straight ahead over a stile.

Carry on for a few hundred yards then the track will bear to the right. This is steep. Further on, go through a hunting gate. Follow the track; it will bear left, winding down to a footbridge. Once over the bridge, bear left. The track will then arc right and go over a stile. Walk straight ahead on a well defined path, keeping close to the right hand boundary. You will start to climb up again, then go through a hunting gate and on the same way, still keeping to the right hand boundary.

Now you benefit from the climb with a good view of the valley, and the village of Brendon. Walk along the ridge and eventually drop down, bearing left, and go through a gate, then on a bit. The path will bend round the top of a combe, up a slope and pass through another gate, then gradually drop down, finally bending to the right, and then take a sharp left turn down to a stile and on to a road. Turn left and follow the road around to a junction. This is Leeford, where accommodation may be found. If you want refreshments, cross the bridge and turn right for the inn at Brendon. Otherwise go past the bridge and walk down about 50 yards to a track on the left. Continue along this track. The village of Brendon is on the other side of the river. You will soon pass through a gate and then between a house and an outbuilding.

A little further on you will find yourself walking on an extremely good path parallel to the river, sometimes near it and at other times

Reproduced from a 1938 Ordnance Survey map.

above it, in an area owned by the National Trust. After a short distance there will be houses on the other side of the river at Alderford. Do not pass through the next gate, but bear right for a short distance up a slope and carry on in the same direction. A lot of these gates and footbridges are private, but this should be quite obvious to the walker, who should just keep to the main track. The woodland here is quite beautiful, mainly oak, with bilberries, ferns, holly and rhododendrons. The river flows over a bed of large rocks, forming quite deep pools. You will eventually go through a small gate. About half a mile distant from Alderford on the other side of the river there is the village of Rockford with its inn, accessible by a public bridge. There is approximately three miles river walking between Leeford and Watersmeet, and you continue on the same track all the way. Sometimes you are about 60 feet above the water, and then you drop down, but always in the same direction. The woodland changes from oak to beech, and there are plenty of mosses, lichens, liverworts and ferns.

Some of the ferns have adapted themselves to grow on the boughs and trunks of the trees. On higher ground heathers may be seen; on lower ground look into the river and see the trout - some quite large. Further on you will come to a small gate and stile, then drop down to a footbridge, but stay on the right hand side of the river. At one point you are on a pinnacle above the river, and way below is a preserved ruin - a quicklime kiln. You will now drop down quite steeply to the riverside again. You are approaching the end of the river walk and entering the area known as Watersmeet. The building here is Watersmeet House, where refreshments are available.

Just past the House, across the bridge, is a diagram giving local information. Cross here, and a few yards to the right go over another bridge from which you will see the Hoaroak Water coming in via a quite spectacular waterfall. Bear right after crossing the second bridge, and up a hill, follow the footpath signs for The Cleaves and continue in a zigzag fashion starting in a series of short turns and carry on until you arrive at a road. Cross straight over the road and take the track opposite. Bear right, still going uphill. Towards the end, the track will swing sharply to the left, coming out into open ground, and straight ahead is another hill to be climbed. You are now at an Iron Age fort - Myrtleberry Camp - amidst bracken, bramble and heather, and some tormentil, with the hills known as the Cleaves ahead. Continue up the hill on a well-defined path, pausing frequently to look back at the views, which become better, the higher, you climb. When the ground starts to level out, you will come to a signpost. Go straight ahead, with a wood on the right, bracken on your left, and probably buzzards soaring above. You will soon come into the open.

Look to the right now - you are at the sea. Down the valley, to the right and ahead, you will see Lynmouth. To its left is Lynton Hill. Out to sea, the coast of Wales may be seen - weather permitting. Continue along the level path on this fine ridge. After a short distance pass through a pair of hunting gates and carry on for about 40 yards. The path then takes a right-hand swing past a stone seat. Drop down, cross a stream and then climb up the other side. Towards the top the ground levels out. Look to the right, down the valley. The oak woods are beautiful, especially in September, with a few tinges of autumn colour, and in summer they are even more spectacular, looking like green cotton wool.

To the right are Foreland Point, and the Church at Countisbury. Soon you will arrive at a signpost saying "Lynbridge". Take that direction, upward to the left. Carry on along a fairly level ridged path, with rowan and oak trees on the right. You are now nearing the end of the Bristol-Lynton section of the walk. As you go down the path, just before it swings to the left, take another look below you at Lynmouth, and Lynton, straight ahead on the opposite hill. Drop down quite steeply on the winding path, pass through a hunting gate, down some steps on the right, keeping to the well-defined path, and cross over a small stream. In summer there are foxgloves, rosebay willowherb, yellow poppies and St. John's wort. Continue to drop down rapidly, pass through the gate and over the

bridge across the River Lyn at Lynbridge. Turn right after the bridge and go up the side of an inn, cross straight over the road into a lane opposite, bearing to the right. At the top of the lane is a three-pronged track. For the Youth Hostel take the middle prong. For Lynton continue down the right hand prong on a good path for approximately a quarter of a mile. At the junction, turn sharp right downhill and keep straight on, then up a few steps to the right to Lynton Church. You have now completed the 100 mile walk from Bristol.

Walk at your own pace - one trip averaged 16 miles a day, but if you decide on 10 miles a day there should be accommodation en route.

You may decide to stop here. It is possible to catch a bus to Barnstaple for connections home by train or bus. Alternatively, you may wish to continue along the North Devon coastal path, firstly to Ilfracombe and then on to Croyde Bay, a distance of some thirty miles, nearly all on National Trust property. On this stretch one may have the good fortune to spot some seals. However the book will not detail this part, as there are already many good books written about it.

THE COASTAL PATH SECTION

LYNTON TO CROYDE BAY - THIRTY MILES OF ONE OF THE MOST DELIGHTFUL STRETCHES OF THE SOUTH WEST PENINSULAR PATH, NEARLY ALL NATIONAL TRUST PROPERTY, BROKEN ONLY BY THE TOWNS OF COMBE MARTIN AND ILFRACOMBE

(Ref: Ordnance Survey Map 180 or Pathfinder Sheet 1214 and 1213) or Explorer 139 and Leisure map No. 9.

A pleasant walk, with completely contrasting landscapes to those you have just enjoyed from Bristol to Lynton. Many authors have already paid tribute to this magnificent section of the coastal path.

You may like to cover the seventeen and a half miles from Lynton to Ilfracombe in one day, leaving a nice easy second day for the walk on to Croyde Bay. However, it is best to split the journey to suit individual needs.

For the coast path when leaving Lynton Church, continue up the hill a short way then turn right beside the old town hall, journeying on through the Valley of Rocks and eventually arriving at Lee Abbey.

From Lee Abbey one can look across Lee Bay to the right. Go on through oak woods above Woody Bay, arriving at Highdeer Point, a very high section of path in open ground. From here look back across superb views to Foreland Point or ahead to Combe Martin Bay. With Heddons Mouth below, drop down into the valley, arriving at a river where a little further on you go over a footbridge. Then brace yourself for a stiff climb to the cliff edges. Prior to the climb, refreshments may be taken at Hunter's Inn a half mile further upstream.

Having now covered about six miles from Lynton, for the next few miles you will go through open countryside before descending into Sherrycombe Valley. Cross over the footbridge and prepare yourself for another steep climb to the top of Great Hangman Hill. At the top there is a huge cairn and a viewpoint from where one can look back and slightly inland, picking out some of the major landmarks across Exmoor.

Drop down from Great Hangman on to Little Hangman and then into the harbour end of the town of Combe Martin, some twelve and a half miles from Lynton. Accommodation may easily be found in Combe Martin, with its two mile length of main street. You may prefer just to take refreshments here and continue the walk, so leave the town by the harbour end and up the hill to rejoin the coastal path to Ilfracombe. Some of the path tends to be near the main road, but before long you come to Watermouth, from where your route will be determined by the height of the tide. Again the route becomes scenic, with a mile or two of small coves below.

On the outskirts of Ilfracombe you arrive at Hele, which has a working corn mill. At this point bear right off the main road. The coastal path will take you to the top of Hillsborough, so you get an excellent view of the town, then descend to the harbour.

Whether you decide to stop for lunch or stay the night, you are spoilt for choice. As well as the Youth Hostel on the terrace at the side of the main road, there are numerous other good eating and resting places.

Having sampled the delights of Ilfracombe, leave the town by working your way round the sea wall towards Torrs Point. With a distance of some twelve and a half miles from Ilfracombe to Croyde Bay, you now continue on National Trust ground with spectacular scenery, passing several bays and points. After three miles you arrive at the village of Lee. Accommodation may be available here, though since it is only a small village advance booking is recommended. A mile further on from Lee, you arrive at Bull Point with its lighthouse. Another mile will bring you to Morte Point - if luck is in this is a likely place to spot seals.

Try to avoid the many side tracks in this area, keeping as near to the sea as is safe, in order to take full advantage of some excellent scenery.

Continue on from Morte Point towards Woolacombe, with its inviting two mile stretch of golden sand. At this point give your boots a rest - They have carried you some 125 miles from Bristol. Let the sea and sand pamper your feet for the next two miles before rebooting for the coastal path again, and on to Baggy Point.

Once around the point, you gradually drop down into Croyde Bay where, sadly, you have come to the end of your walk from Bristol.

I'm sure you will want to show your appreciation to the National Trust for its tremendous work in preserving the natural beauties of the coast. Please give generously at the NT box and refresh yourself with a pot of tea from one of the hotels or beach shops.

The Way Home

You may wish to carry on walking the South West Coastal path. After all there is another 450 miles to Poole Harbour. Alternatively you may wish to have a rest and go on home. A local bus from Croyde Bay, or a little further on from Croyde Bridge will take you to Barnstaple. Stay the night, or travel home the same day. Barnstaple is well serve by trains and buses.

The local buses can be few and far between, so check the timetables. There are information offices at major towns along the coast.

On the way back and if travelling by bus, look out for some of the main landmarks such as the ridges of the Quantock and Polden Hills. Watch out for the little footbridge over the M5 then the Mendip Hills. Lastly the Clifton Suspension Bridge.

Suggested Accommodation Guides

Ramblers' Year Book and Accommodation Guide

The Ramblers' Association
1/5 Wandsworth Road
London SW8 2XX

The Youth Hostels Association Accommodation Guide

YHA
Trevelyan House
8 St Stephens Hill
St Albans
Herts
AL1 2DY

Membership of RA and YHA well worthwhile - both Registered Charities

Available hostels: Bristol
                           Cheddar
                           Street
                           Exford
                           Lynton
                           Ilfracombe